TALES OF HEAVEN AND EARTH

Michelle Esclapez taught French
in southern India for many years.
She is the author of several books
about Indian legends.

Cover design by Peter Bennett

ISBN: 1 85103 257 6
© Editions Gallimard, 1995
Managing editor: Jacqueline Vallon
Adviser for UK edition: Professor Raychaudhuri, retired Professor of Indian History,
Oxford University, and Emeritus Fellow at St Anthony's College, Oxford.
English text © 1996 by Moonlight Publishing Ltd
First published in the United Kingdom 1997
by Moonlight Publishing Ltd, 36 Stratford Road, London W8
Printed in Italy by Editoriale Zanardi

RAMA, THE HEROIC PRINCE

by Michelle Esclapez

Illustrated by Marie Mallard

Translated by Simona Sideri

Moonlight Publishing

*For Allison,
Lorène and Dorothée*

According to Indian tradition, the *Ramayana* was written by Valmiki, a mythical sage. His meeting with the sage Narada changed his life. He became an ascetic, living a simple life of prayer and discipline. One day he entered into a meditation so deep that thousands of ants crawled all over him without his noticing. His name, Valmiki, given him by Narada, means son of the anthill in Sanskrit.

Long, long ago the poet Valmiki turned to the old sage Narada and asked, "Blessed Narada, can you tell me if there is any man on this earth today who is just and good, pure in his beliefs, strong and constant in the practice of virtue? Is there anyone who is truly noble, who knows how to be helpful to others while remaining in control of himself, a free spirit before whom even the gods bow down? Tell me, oh venerable singer, if you know of such a man?"

Narada, who had journeyed through all three worlds,

The Hindus venerate three major gods – Brahma the creator, Vishnu the protector and Shiva the destroyer – as well as many others.

The three worlds are the Heavens, the Earth and the Underworld. The sage studies every aspect of the Universe.

Rishis are sages to whom the gods have taught the meaning of the sacred texts. (Above, an ascetic, from a 16th-century sculpture.)

To Hindus and Buddhists the lotus represents purity and wisdom. Just as the sage is not attached to earthly pleasures, so the lotus roots plunge into water, its flower rising above the surface.

In Asia the elephant stands for strength, majesty and peace.

answered, "Great rishi, such a man does indeed exist. He is of the royal line of Ikshvaku, his name is Rama and he is truly a hero." Taking up his vina he began to sing:

"For his feet are as lotus flowers
And his step is like that of a young elephant.
Dressed in yellow cloth,
Round his waist a golden chain is hung with jewels.
Tall and broad-chested,
His neck is as elegant as a conch shell,
His skin the colour of rain clouds.
He is radiant as the lotus, splendid as the tamal tree.
His face is more beautiful than the moon herself."

When Narada had finished Valmiki thanked him and retired to the banks of the river Tamasa where he bathed and purified himself. As he meditated in the forest the god Brahma, creator of the three worlds, appeared before him. "Valmiki," he commanded, "go and tell the world the story of Rama, tell of the exploits of this great hero, as Narada told you. Never stop praising Rama, his courage, his goodness, his bravery, his gentleness."

And so the great rishi Valmiki began to recount the adventures of Rama-of-the-lotus-eyes.

On the banks of the river Sarayu stood the wealthy city of

Ikshvaku, the grandson of the Sun (the god Surya) was the first in the royal line of Ayodhya.

Yellow is the colour of the Sun and eternity. Rama is an incarnation of Vishnu who is always dressed in yellow.

The vina is a stringed instrument from Southern India. It is said to have been first made by Narada.

The conch shell was blown as a call to battle.

Rama's blue skin recalls the ocean depths.

6

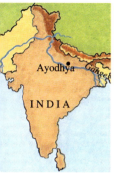

Ayodhya ruled by King Dasharatha, who was greatly loved by his people. As was sometimes the way in those days long gone, Dasharatha had three wives, Kaushalya, Kaikeyi and Sumitra. Dasharatha had been childless for many years but then, much to his joy, his wives had given birth. The eldest child was Rama, son of Kaushalya. The beautiful Kaikeyi was the mother of Bharata. While the young queen Sumitra gave birth to twins named Lakshmana and Satrughna. The four brothers were devoted to each other and loved their father greatly. They were taught the sacred texts as well as all the arts, including the martial arts. All four were noble and accomplished, but Rama's radiant beauty and courteous disposition caused him to shine out. Lakshmana, who worshipped his elder brother, could not bear to be separated from him.

One day, when the princes were about sixteen, Vishwamitra came to the court. He was warmly welcomed, as was due a famous rajarshi, by Dasharatha himself, who asked, perhaps unwisely, "Why are you here, holy man? How can we be of service to you? I will gladly offer you whatever you desire." Vishwamitra answered with a slow smile. "I have been making a sacrifice to the gods, but evil rakshasa put out my sacred

The ancient city of Ayodhya was the capital of the kingdom of Kosala. With hundreds of temples it is still today one of the seven sacred cities of the Hindus. It is also holy to Buddhists, as the Buddha preached there for six years.

A rajarshi is a king who has given up his realm to live like an ascetic, praying in the forest.

Brahma is also known as Padmanabha, born of the lotus flower. Above, he emerges from a lotus flower rooted in Vishnu's belly button. Vishnu reclines on the snake (eternity) which floats on the ancient ocean.

And so Valmiki began his story.

fire and stopped me from continuing. Let your son Rama come with me into the forest to keep these demons away and allow me to continue my prayers."

Dasharatha was dismayed by these words but, unwilling to cross the holy man, he murmured, "Rama is only a child. How could he help you? I will go myself with all my armies, but don't ask Rama to go."

At this Vishwamitra flew into a rage. How dare the King refuse him! "You asked me what I wanted! I want Rama and nobody else will do!" he thundered.

Then the King's adviser, the sage Vasishtha, spoke up. "Do not fear for Rama my King, he will be safe with Vishwamitra." And so, with a heavy heart, Dasharatha watched Rama leave, followed as always by Lakshmana.

The young princes were delighted at the prospect of an adventure. Vishwamitra proved an excellent teacher and on the way taught them all he knew about the art of war. The journey was full of danger and excitement. When a fearsome demon attacked Rama, he killed it with all the skill of a seasoned warrior. Vishwamitra, proud of his pupil, made Rama a gift of holy weapons which, as he knew already, the prince would need to accomplish the tasks that lay ahead.

Finally they arrived at the place where the rishis were

Above, an altar for sacrificial fires. Sacrifices are performed to appease the gods, and keep their goodwill. They only work if the strict rules are followed, and the proceedings are not interrupted. The priest, or brahmin, lights the fire, and feeds it with various offerings while chanting the sacred words or mantras.

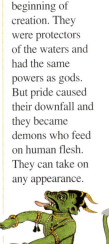

Rakshasa are believed to have been made by Brahma at the beginning of creation. They were protectors of the waters and had the same powers as gods. But pride caused their downfall and they became demons who feed on human flesh. They can take on any appearance.

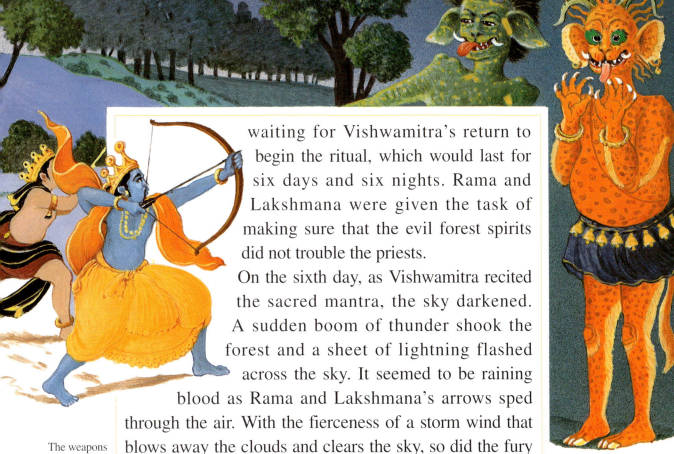

waiting for Vishwamitra's return to begin the ritual, which would last for six days and six nights. Rama and Lakshmana were given the task of making sure that the evil forest spirits did not trouble the priests.

On the sixth day, as Vishwamitra recited the sacred mantra, the sky darkened. A sudden boom of thunder shook the forest and a sheet of lightning flashed across the sky. It seemed to be raining blood as Rama and Lakshmana's arrows sped through the air. With the fierceness of a storm wind that blows away the clouds and clears the sky, so did the fury of their arrows chase away the dangerous rakshasa. One fell into the sea and another was killed outright. That was enough to put the rest to flight and Vishwamitra finished his ritual in peace. Afterwards he blessed the princes, while the holy men gathered round and thanked them from the depths of their hearts.

The next morning Vishwamitra announced some news. "Janaka, the king of Videha, is holding a great festival. He owns a bow so mighty that no-one has yet been able to raise it! Let us go and see this famous bow and take

The weapons Vishwamitra gives Rama are gifts from the gods. They are fired by the energy of goodness, justice and truth. They must be used by the right person and with the correct mantras. Rama will need these weapons in later battles against the demons.

The huge bow once belonged to the god Shiva and no-one, neither god nor human had ever been able to lift it. The fact that Rama was actually able to break it is a sign that he is indeed a god. Buddhists believe that the Buddha performed the same feat.

Rama was a handsome prince beloved of all.

Rama the archer
(from an 18th-
century painting)

part in the ceremony."

King Janaka soon noticed the handsome young men who had arrived at the court with Vishwamitra and asked the old man who they were. "They radiate light like the Sun and Moon themselves," he murmured in awe.

"They are the sons of King Dasharatha and have helped me make my ritual offering," answered the sage. "We have come to see your mighty bow."

"Then they should know that I will give the hand of my dear daughter Sita in marriage to the prince who draws the bow. Many have tried, but none has succeeded. It is an ancient bow that has been in my family for centuries. But come, let me show you." A crowd gathered round as Rama and Lakshmana examined the bow.

Vishwamitra motioned Rama to step forward. "Pick it up, my child."

Rama turned respectfully towards the bow and picked it up with apparent ease. As he bent it back and drew the string, the huge bow cracked and split in two. Janaka was overjoyed. Here was a man worthy of his daughter!

As the people of Mithila gathered to celebrate, messengers were sent to Dasharatha, inviting him to the marriage of his son Rama and the beautiful Sita.

Many years before, during a long period of famine, King Janaka decided to offer a sacrifice to the gods. As he was marking out the place where the sacrifice would be made, his plough stopped in its tracks: a little girl was sitting in the furrow. Janaka, who had no children of his own, took the child to his queen who welcomed her. She named the girl Sita, meaning furrow. Born of the earth, Sita was often venerated as a fertility goddess in ancient times.

He had many adventures.

Sita,
Rama's wife.

Ever since he had watched his
sons leave with Vishwamitra,
Dasharatha had worried for their
safety. His fears had led him to believe that they had been
defeated by the forest demons and were probably dead.
He was overjoyed to hear the good news. He immediately set off for Videha with his wives and other sons.
On their arrival the happy families congratulated each
other and exchanged rich gifts. The marriage was
celebrated in great pomp and splendour. Later, Rama and
Sita returned to Ayodhya where the people lined the
streets to greet them with flowers and more presents.

Rama was to be crowned King of Ayodhya.

Vishnu and some of his avatars, or incarnations, have blue skin. Below, Vishnu as the fish, Matsya, from an 18th-century carving.

The peacock is India's national bird. The wheels on its brilliant tail feathers make it a symbol of the Sun and it is linked to drought. Traditional rain dances are known as peacock dances. Below, a Moghul miniature.

Twelve years passed, twelve years of true peace and happiness during which Rama became famed for his compassion and fairness. The people loved him dearly. Then, one day, Dasharatha assembled his ministers. "I have governed to the best of my ability until this day," he told them. "Now it is time that Prince Rama, who has shown himself worthy of your respect, should become King." A murmur of approval was heard. And when the people of Ayodhya were told the news they greeted their Prince, the virtuous Rama-of-the-blue-skin, with joyful shrieks, like peacocks when they see rain clouds

But jealous Kaikeyi demanded that Bharata be king.

Below, Kaikeyi, who caused Rama to be exiled.

Some years before, Kaikeyi had been with the king when he had fought the demon Sambara. Dasharatha had been wounded and lost consciousness but Kaikeyi, showing no fear, had driven his chariot off the battle field, removed the arrow from his body and staunched the bleeding. In gratitude the king had granted her three wishes.

gathering in the sky.

Everyone was delighted at the news that Rama was to be King, everyone except Kaikeyi, Bharata's mother. Proud and selfish, she listened to the malicious plot hatched by her wily, hunchbacked servant, Manthara. "Bharata should be King by rights!" the maid hissed in her ear. "Now he will merely be Rama's servant, and you nothing but a slave!"

That night when Dasharatha visited Kaikeyi he found her on the floor crying in pain. Thinking she was ill, he tried to comfort her, but she pushed him away roughly.

"Do you remember the three wishes you granted me when I nursed your battle wounds long ago?" she asked him threateningly. "Of course," answered Dasharatha. "What can I give you, my dearest queen, to make you happy?" "Let Bharata be crowned king," she answered harshly, "and banish Rama from the kingdom for fourteen years to live the life of an ascetic in the forest."

Dasharatha could not believe his ears: Kaikeyi was asking for Rama's exile, Rama who had never harmed a soul!

13

So Rama was exiled, for the King must keep his word.

He was angry. "Have you gone mad, woman?" he roared. But Kaikeyi stubbornly refused to change her mind. At daybreak, when the chief minister, Sumantra, came to announce that all was ready for Rama's coronation, he found the King in Kaikeyi's rooms, in despair. "Send Rama to me immediately," Kaikeyi ordered. Rama listened patiently to what she had to say and then, without a shadow of reproach, he spoke in a calm voice. "Let Bharata be crowned. Nothing should stand in the way of my father's promise to you. I will leave for the forest this very day." "Perfect," hissed Kaikeyi. "The sooner the better!" Hearing these words Dasharatha cried out in disbelief, "Have you no shame, you miserable wretch?" and then he fainted.

Rama went to his mother, Kaushalya, who was at her prayers, and Lakshmana told her the bad news.

"Then let me come with you," pleaded Kaushalya. "No," Rama answered, "father will need you more than ever now." And with this Kaushalya had to agree. Then Lakshmana spoke. In a tone allowing for no discussion he announced, "I will go with Rama and look after him. Let no-one stop me."

Meanwhile, Sita had been waiting for her Lord, to admire him in his royal robes. But one look at his face told her

In Hindu philosophy a wise man learns not to feel anger and not to react emotionally to events.

something was wrong and she ran into his arms. "What has happened, beloved?" she asked. "Daughter of Janaka, my father has banished me from the kingdom for fourteen years. I am to live as an exile in the forest, while Bharata is to be crowned today in my place. This is not the wish of the King, my father, but he is bound by a promise made long ago, and must accept this, as I do. I must go now dearest. Do nothing to displease Bharata while I am not here." Despite her sweet nature, Sita became furious. "Why do you speak to me like this? Shouldn't a wife share her husband's fate? I want nothing more than to be with you. If you leave me behind I will kill myself." Rama begged her to change her mind, reminding her how hard life in the forest would be. But Sita remained firm and Rama had to grant her wish. And in his heart he was glad that she would go with him.

So it was that Rama, Sita and Lakshmana exchanged their royal clothes for the simple garb of hermits. They bade farewell to the distraught King and to the despairing queens and left the city of Ayodhya. Unable to look back for fear of losing his resolve, Rama implored their coachman, the minister Sumantra, to drive faster and faster. It was only when they reached the banks of the river Tamasa that he agreed to stop.

Below, Kaushalya, Rama's mother.

Hermits wear simple, rough clothing, sometimes even made from the bark of trees.

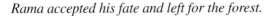

Rama accepted his fate and left for the forest.

3

Rama, Sita and Lakshmana began their journey through the forest of Chitrakuta and gradually the tranquillity of the surroundings brought peace to their troubled spirits. Rama-of-the-lotus-eyes smiled tenderly at Sita. "Look dearest, this is where the Mandakini flows. The trees along its banks are heavy with fruit and lotus flowers grow from its depths. Here the whole forest echoes with the gentle song of the cuckoo and fawns come to quench their thirst. Vines snake lovingly around mango trees and look, there is even a cave for us to shelter in."

Chitrakuta, where Valmiki is believed to have lived, could be modern day Chitrakote, near Banda in Uttar Pradesh. It is a holy place visited by many pilgrims.

According to the rules of Sanskrit poetry people's names are often followed by brief epithets (descriptions of their qualities). This technique was also used by Homer in the *Iliad* and the *Odyssey*.

Mandakini is a name for the part of the Ganges flowing through the heavens. But here the reference is also to a river in Bundelkhand, Uttar Pradesh, perhaps the river known now as the Pisuni.

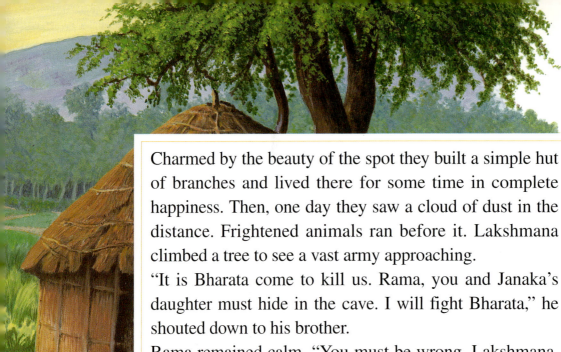

Charmed by the beauty of the spot they built a simple hut of branches and lived there for some time in complete happiness. Then, one day they saw a cloud of dust in the distance. Frightened animals ran before it. Lakshmana climbed a tree to see a vast army approaching.

"It is Bharata come to kill us. Rama, you and Janaka's daughter must hide in the cave. I will fight Bharata," he shouted down to his brother.

Rama remained calm. "You must be wrong, Lakshmana. What use is a kingdom conquered by force? And surely Bharata loves me dearly? Perhaps he has come with father."

At the head of the army marched Bharata and his brother Satrughna, accompanied by the sage Vasishtha and the three queens. When he reached the hut, Bharata hugged his brother, but there was sadness in the embrace. As Rama hugged him back neither could speak through their tears. Finally Rama asked, "Where is father? You should not have left him alone."

Bharata answered in a voice overcome with emotion. "Father died six days after you left. He could not endure the pain of your departure." Hearing this Rama fell to the ground and sobbed. The brave and heroic Rama was felled by this cruel blow to his heart. Sita, also in tears,

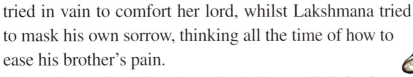
His brother Lakshmana and wife Sita travelled with him.

Duty – to one's father, for example, is thought of as a moral law, dharma, to which all must conform. Dharma represents the harmony of the universe. Rama is considered the great champion of dharma.

By putting Rama's sandals on the throne, Bharata wanted to demonstrate his own total subjection to Rama. (Above, a 1st-century sculpture.)

tried in vain to comfort her lord, whilst Lakshmana tried to mask his own sorrow, thinking all the time of how to ease his brother's pain.

The next morning Bharata spoke to Rama. "My lord, I beg you to return to your kingdom. Only then will I be liberated from the great shame that I feel."

"Bharata," Rama replied, "you must do your duty and I must do mine. We must keep father's word. I will fulfil our father's promise even should the moon's light fade or the snow on the peaks of the Himalayas melt. So, look after the kingdom well, my brother."

Bharata listened to his words without any expression, but he was greatly moved and asked, "Oh Lord, then give me your sandals, for they will protect our people." When Rama had given them to him he continued. "I will place these sandals on the throne and I vow that for fourteen years I will only wear the bark clothes of hermits. I will undertake my duties as regent, but I vow never to enter our city, Ayodhya. If you have not returned on the first day of the fifteenth year, I will throw myself into the fire." Thus spoke the noble Bharata.

On his return to Ayodhya he placed Rama's sandals on the throne and ruled the country from Nandigram, a nearby village, where he made his home.

They built a bamboo hut and lived like hermits.

Sita and the princes met many hermits and ascetics who complained of the cruelty of the rakshasa. "Rama," they begged, "you are lord of this forest yet many of us have lost our lives due to the strength of these demons. Deliver us from this threat, we beg you." And so Rama promised to protect them.

After Bharata had left Rama was no longer able to enjoy the peace of Chitrakuta and he made his way to the forest of Dandaka. Soon our three heroes reached the abode of the sage Agastya, famous both for his great knowledge and for his holiness. Rama greeted the sage, who embraced him and gave him a bow and a sword with a silver scabbard, weapons he had himself been given by Vishnu. The holy man advised them to settle in Panchavati and blessed them before they left. On arriving Lakshmana built a new hut, of bamboo and dried mud, under the fruit trees.

Below, a picture of a wandering ascetic, wearing his hair in a bun to show he has given up all worldly things. He holds the sacred texts in one hand and a rosary in the other (from an 18th-century painting).

Their new home
looked over the
river Godavari, along whose banks
many animals gathered to drink. For
a while they lived in perfect contentment,
forgetting their sorrow once more in the beauty
surrounding them. The winter months were cold,
but they had grown used to it by now.

"During this season the forest is thick with mist and the thirsty elephants shy away from the icy water," mused Lakshmana. "The midday sun is as pale as the moon and the lotus have lost their petals." Such thoughts led him back to Ayodhya. "I wonder if Bharata is bathing in the cold waters of the Sarayu with our people..."

"Will we ever see him again?" wondered Rama. "May the Gods guide us."

Winter passed and spring came, bringing them a visitor. It was a beautiful woman who at the first glimpse of Rama fell in love with him. "Who are you?" she asked him. "And what are you doing here, such a handsome young man as you, dressed in the simple clothes of a hermit?"

Rama told her who he was and asked where she hailed from. "I am Shurpanakha, the sister of Ravana, the

Ravana is invincible. After a long period of penance and spiritual discipline, he is able to convince Brahma to make him invulnerable to the powers both of the gods and of other demons. However, in his pride he forgets to ask for protection against people and animals (except for snakes and birds). That is why Vishnu has to take on human form, in the person of Rama, to defeat Ravana.

Place names used in the *Ramayana* do not always match modern names. So Lanka may or may not be Sri-Lanka, or some other distant place.

unbeatable. From the moment I set eyes on you I knew you were meant to be my lord."

Rama smiled, pointing to Sita. "This is Sita, my beloved wife." And then to tease her he added, "but here is Lakshmana, my brother. You could marry him."

Before their very eyes the beautiful woman turned into a screaming demon and attacked Sita. Rama quickly stepped forward to protect his beloved, while Lakshmana pulled out his sword and sliced off the demon's ears and nose. Humiliated and in agony, she returned to Lanka to demand revenge. Her brother, Ravana, King of the demons, was delighted by the prospect and persuaded his uncle Maricha to help. Reluctantly, Maricha agreed to go to Panchavati disguised as a beautiful doe with a shimmering coat of such beauty that Sita would be unable to resist its charm.

Wandering alone in the forest Sita caught sight of the doe. What a beautiful golden animal! She tried to entice it, but the doe kept its distance warily.

"Come quickly," she called to Rama. "Look at that beautiful deer. Would you catch her for me?"

"Take care that it is not a rakshasa in disguise," Lakshmana warned, his

Rama, Sita and Lakshmana, holding the demon Shurpanakha by her hair (from a Gupta carving of the 5th century).

Maricha had faced Rama in battle years before and was terrified of him. He knows the demons cannot defeat Rama.

Ravana, demon King of Lanka, was plotting against Sita.

A sadhu is an ascetic, a religious person who fasts, prays and meditates. They generally dress in saffron coloured robes and carry a pilgrim's stick and a wooden bowl. They live by begging. In ancient India sadhus were highly respected and it was everyone's duty to give them alms. Disguised as a sadhu, Ravana knows he will be well received by Sita.

suspicions aroused.

Sita would not believe this and pleaded more, so Rama set off after the deer, leaving Lakshmana to guard his wife.

The doe sped through the forest and, realising he was never going to catch it alive, Rama fired an arrow. The doe fell, wounded, but it soon revealed that it was no ordinary deer, for it began to call for help using Rama's voice. "Lakshmana. Help! Help!" Far away, Sita heard the cry and feared Rama was in danger. She begged Lakshmana to go to his aid. Lakshmana tried to calm her fears. "It's a trick. No rakshasa can beat Rama. He will be here any moment and I must not leave you alone."

But Sita became so angry that Lakshmana was forced to do as she asked. He drew a circle around the hut to keep her safe and begged her under no circumstance to step outside it.

Ravana's plan was working well and Sita was alone now. Dressed as a sadhu, the demon approached the hut where Sita greeted him with respect. Her beauty and grace enchanted him, for even in her simple dress she looked like a goddess. "You are far too beautiful to live in such a poor hut. Why and how have you come to be here?" he asked in the gentle voice of the holy man.

According to legend, Indra was taken prisoner by Ravana's son during a war between the gods and the demons. From that moment the demon was known as Indrajita, or Indra's vanquisher. Below, Indra on his elephant, Airavata (13th-century sculpture).

23

Overwhelmed by her beauty he carried her away.

Garuda, king
of the birds (from
an 18th-century
painting).

Jatayu is the chief
vulture and son
of Garuda, the
fabulous bird
ridden by Vishnu.
He is an old
friend of King
Dasharatha.

Sita, still believing him to be what he seemed, told him her story. As he listened the sadhu slowly changed back into his demon form. "Come with me," he screeched, "I will make you queen of Lanka. I am Ravana, King of the rakshasa, feared throughout the world."

Sita was horrified by this suggestion. "I am Rama's wife," she cried. "How dare you ask me to be your queen. Go at once!" But in her indignation she forgot Lakshmana's warning and stepped out of his magic circle. As she did so Ravana saw his chance. He took her to his chariot and drove away into the skies. No-one was at hand to help. But as the chariot passed, the vulture Jatayu heard her piteous cries. He flew bravely at the chariot, attacking Ravana with his beak. But the rakshasa overpowered him and chopped off his wings. The mighty bird was dashed to the ground and lay bleeding where he fell.

Ravana is
described in
the *Ramayana*
as a terrifying
creature with 10
heads, 20 arms,
eyes as red as
copper and teeth
as white as the
moon.
He is
said to
be as tall
as a mountain,
and he only
needs to stretch
out his arm to
pull the Sun
or the Moon
off course.

Hanuman, the monkey warrior, came to Rama's aid.

Hanuman is the son of the Wind god, Vayu, and of an apsara (a heavenly nymph) who had been changed into a monkey by a curse. He is immortal. He has the power to grow or shrink, and can fly. In Hindu tradition Hanuman is revered as a sage and a devotee of Rama and Sita, for whom he has a boundless love.
He himself is much revered by the people and there is a temple dedicated to him at Ayodhya.

On their return, Rama and Lakshmana found the hut empty and Sita gone. They searched high and low, but there was no sign of her. It was only when they came upon the dying Jatayu that they learned that she had been kidnapped by the king of the rakshasas and carried off toward the south in his chariot.

Immediately Rama and Lakshmana set off to find her. After much travelling they reached Lake Pampa, where they stopped to rest. In the nearby hills lived Sugriva, the exiled king of the monkeys of Kishkindha, with his followers. Spying the two travellers he sent Hanuman, his

Kishkindha is the kingdom of the monkeys. Their king, Sugriva, lives in exile, having been chased from his kingdom by his brother Vali. Another story from the *Ramayana* tells how Rama kills Vali and returns the kingdom to Sugriva. Below, Sugriva's coronation (from an 18th-century painting).

25

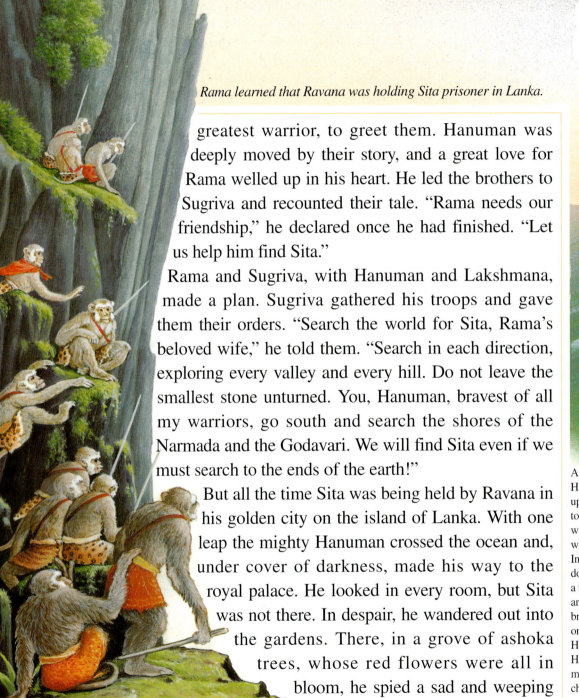

Rama learned that Ravana was holding Sita prisoner in Lanka.

greatest warrior, to greet them. Hanuman was deeply moved by their story, and a great love for Rama welled up in his heart. He led the brothers to Sugriva and recounted their tale. "Rama needs our friendship," he declared once he had finished. "Let us help him find Sita."

Rama and Sugriva, with Hanuman and Lakshmana, made a plan. Sugriva gathered his troops and gave them their orders. "Search the world for Sita, Rama's beloved wife," he told them. "Search in each direction, exploring every valley and every hill. Do not leave the smallest stone unturned. You, Hanuman, bravest of all my warriors, go south and search the shores of the Narmada and the Godavari. We will find Sita even if we must search to the ends of the earth!"

But all the time Sita was being held by Ravana in his golden city on the island of Lanka. With one leap the mighty Hanuman crossed the ocean and, under cover of darkness, made his way to the royal palace. He looked in every room, but Sita was not there. In despair, he wandered out into the gardens. There, in a grove of ashoka trees, whose red flowers were all in bloom, he spied a sad and weeping

As a youth Hanuman leapt up into the sky to pick the sun, which he thought was a ripe fruit. Indra struck him down with a thunderbolt and as he fell he broke his chin on a mountain. He was named Hanuman, meaning large chin.

face, whose beauty shone amongst those of the ugly demons watching over her.

"That must be Sita," he told himself. "The tears of her sorrow have not dulled her beauty," and he settled down to wait for the moon to rise and the demons to fall asleep.

It was indeed Sita, but how unhappy she looked! Ravana had worn her down with his determination to marry her. And when he wasn't terrorising her with his threats the demons sang his praises to the unfortunate Sita, until she had almost abandoned any hope of her lord Rama coming to save her.

Seeing Hanuman creeping towards her, Sita trembled with fear, but the monkey warrior spoke gently to her. "I come from Rama," he said. "Do not fear me. See, I bring you his ring, which he sends with all his love."

Sita was overjoyed at the news. She asked Hanuman countless questions about Rama and then gave him a jewel from her hair, saying, "Take this, Hanuman, and give it to my dear lord. Tell him that I think of him constantly and pray that he will deliver me soon."

Hanuman set off back to Rama, but as he made his way through the city he was

The ashoka is a tree bearing red flowers. They are thought to be home to Kama, god of love, and are themselves symbols of passion and love. That is why Sita sat in the ashoka grove and thought of Rama.

The forest animals brought wood and stones.

The word vanara comes from the Sanskrit vana, forest, and is used to mean the animals of the forest, especially monkeys. In the *Ramayana* this word is used to describe the army of monkeys Sugriva puts at Rama's disposal.

Hanuman crosses the ocean in one mighty leap (from an 18th-century painting).

captured and taken to Ravana. The sight of the rakshasa King and the evil demons around him awed Hanuman at first. He made his body grow larger and larger! Then he spoke these words of warning. "Return Sita to her lord or you will cause the ruin of yourself and your people. I am Rama's messenger and I say this for your own good." This made Ravana furious and he called his guards. "Set fire to this proud vanara's tail. Parade him through the city in flames for all to see."

Instantly the rakshasa wrapped the monkey's huge tail in strips of cloth dipped in oil, and set fire to it. As they did so, Hanuman grew even larger before their very eyes and his blazing tail thrashed violently in all directions. In fear of their lives the rakshasa fled. Like a streak of lightning, Hanuman leapt from house to house, until the whole of Lanka was burning. Then he plunged his tail in to the ocean to quench the fire and hurried back to Rama with the joyful news of Sita's whereabouts.

Deep in thought, Rama listened in silence to Hanuman's story while stroking the jewel Sita had sent him. He and Lakshmana both exchanged looks of heartfelt gratitude with this mighty monkey warrior.

When Hanuman had rested and regained his strength, he stood before Sugriva's army. "Let us go now and conquer

Rama, Lakshmana and Hanuman (18th-century Indian painting).

They built a bridge so the army could cross the ocean.

Lanka," he cried. The thousands of monkeys roared their approval. They were ready for war.

With the help of all the forest animals, even the gentle squirrels, a mighty bridge of stones, bushes, rocks and trees was built over the ocean to Lanka. Rama and his army set off across the bridge.

Squirrels are sacred in India. The dark lines on their stripey coats were reputedly made by Rama's fingers as he stroked them.

Rama's army of monkeys and bears was ready to fight.

Vibhishana, Ravana's brother, advised him to return Sita to Rama to avoid war. Faced with his brother's stubbornness he took Rama's side and fought alongside him. After Ravana's death Rama gave him the throne of Lanka. Below Rama, Lakshmana and Vibhishana hold council, surrounded by the army of monkeys and bears.

Ravana had been forewarned of Rama's attack by his brother, Vibhishana, and by several of his ministers. They had all advised him to return Sita and make peace with Rama, but he had not listened to them. Soon the armies were drawn up and the battle could begin.

Rama, Lakshmana and the monkeys and bears of Sugriva's army fought valiantly. But Ravana used all his magic powers to sow panic amongst them and brought down a thick fog to blind them. Yet Rama's army kept the upper hand and soon many of the strongest rakshasa were killed. Amongst them was the giant Kumbhakarna,

Below, Ravana asking the advice of the demon-ascetic Maricha.

Kumbhakarna, brother of Ravana, is a giant. He was cursed by Brahma to sleep all the time except for one day every six months when he wakes up to consume huge quantities of food.

one of Ravana's brothers, and his favourite son Indrajita. It was then that Ravana hurled his supreme weapon, a magical javelin given to him by Brahma. It flew through the air like a blazing streak of light to hit Lakshmana.

The young prince fell, mortally wounded, and only one herb in the whole world could heal him now. Hanuman was sent to find it. Arriving on the hill where the life-giving plant grew, he was unable to recognise it. Not wishing to lose any more time he picked up the hill itself and, holding it in one hand, brought it to Rama. Lakshmana was healed and able to fight again, but Rama knew the end was near.

The next day he placed himself at the forefront of the battle to take on Ravana face to face. This fight was just one stage in the endless war that has raged between the forces of good and evil from time immemorial. The sky darkened. Jackals and vultures filled the air with their mournful cries, as the final struggle began between Rama and Ravana. Even the gods are said to have watched from the skies above. Ravana's ten arms sent a blaze of arrows

Indrajita, Ravana's son, is a magician and can make himself invisible. Lakshmana kills him with an arrow from Indra's bow.

31

Finally Rama took up his divine bow and killed Ravana.

towards Rama from all sides. Oblivious to any pain, Rama fired back his own steady torrent.

Both were determined to triumph, at any price, and called on all their strength. As a last resort Rama picked up the bow given to him by the sage Agastya, a mighty weapon which had belonged to Brahma himself. The arrow flew straight into the heart of the king of the demons, who fell instantly. Proud Ravana, arrogant king of the rakshasa, lay with his nose in the dust. Bellowing loudly, the vanaras raised their hands in thanks for their victory.

The wind swept gently over the battlefield and the earth itself sighed and rejoiced. A heavenly voice was heard to whisper, "Rama, your mission is done!" Rama turned solemnly to Sita. "Daughter of Janaka," he began, "after your long stay in Ravana's palace I cannot take you back as my wife."

These cold, cruel words slid like a knife into Sita's heart, but she collected herself and turned to Lakshmana. "So be it! Prepare a funeral pyre that I may throw myself upon it." A huge pyre was laid and, when it was lit, Sita walked towards it and threw herself into the flames. As these died away Agni, god of fire, appeared with Sita in his

After his victory, Brahma comes down to tell Rama of his divine origins: "You are Narayana (Vishnu) armed with the chakra. You are the truth without beginning or end. You are the dharma which rules the world. Sita is Devi Lakshmi (wife of Vishnu) and you are Vishnu, born on Earth to destroy Ravana. Your mission is accomplished and dharma has been re-established."

Indra sends down a chariot for Rama, driven by his own charioteer. This gift, with all the other weapons and teachings he has received from the gods, enables Rama finally to vanquish Ravana.

32

arms, looking more beautiful than ever. He led her to Rama saying, "Here is Sita, your beloved, know that she is pure and faithful." Rama took her. "I never doubted you, my love," he told her, "but the whole world had to be sure of your purity." Sita said nothing, but was happy.

The people of Ayodhya were overjoyed when they heard of Rama's and Sita's return. When the crowds caught sight of the heavenly chariot, once Ravana's, they cheered with pleasure, and the echo spread across the world like peals of thunder. Bharata put the golden sandals back on Rama's feet. "I return your throne to you, oh my king," he announced. "May you live in peace for many years!"

Still today when people in India talk of an enlightened rule they call it Rama Rajya, the reign of Rama.

In a third section added later to Valmiki's original poem, the people of Ayodhya are not fully convinced by Sita's trial by fire and force her to leave the city. She shelters in the forest and gives birth to twins who travel the world recounting the *Ramayana*. They reach the court of their father, who instantly recognises them. Rama begs Sita to return to the palace, but she, exhausted by hardship, asks her mother, the Earth, to take her back into her bosom.

Agni (the word shares the root with the Latin word ignis, fire) was one of the main gods of ancient India. He was much revered and his role during a sacrifice was as messenger between gods and humans. He was the protector of people.

The *Ramayana* continues with Rama's coronation amid happiness. Legend has it that Rama ruled for 11,000 years. He was a just ruler and his reign was a time of peace and prosperity.

A kathakali actor
playing the role
of Rama.

Who is Rama?

The *Ramayana* is a tale of adventure and heroic deeds, a love story and an initiation all at once. Rama is a prince and a warrior who follows the path of honour and duty – dharma – which raises him above all petty personal feelings. His marriage to Sita has come to symbolise the union of the soul (Sita) with the divine (Rama) and the difficulties they face are the necessary obstacles on the path to wisdom. The painful experiences Rama must contend with (exile, the death of his father) and the gifts and knowledge he receives along the way help him become a better person and realise his divine potential.

Vishnu's avatar

At the start of the *Ramayana*, the Earth complains to the gods of its miserable state. They in turn ask Vishnu, in his role as protector, to go down to Earth in human form (to incarnate). So Rama comes to be born. He is Vishnu become man and his mission is to protect humanity against the evil rakshasa which threaten to overrun the Earth.

The ten incarnations of Vishnu

According to Indian tradition, Vishnu has many avatars. These are the ten most important ones:
– Matsya, the fish, saved humanity and the *Vedas* from the flood.
– Kurma the tortoise
– Varaha the boar
– Narasimha the lion-man, delivered the world from a demon.
– Vamana the dwarf, restored the three worlds to the gods, the demons and humankind.
– Parashurama, who reinstated the caste of brahmins.
– Rama
– Krishna
– Buddha, the founder of Buddhism.
– Kalki, a knight riding a white horse, who is still awaited.

Centre: Brahma and his daughter Sarasvati sit on a lotus flower. Brahma has four heads and holds the *Vedas*. These are said to have been brought into being by his very breath and written down by rishis (from a painting of the end of the 18th century).

The sacred texts of Hinduism

Fertility goddess (pottery statuette from the 1st century BC).

The *Ramayana* was first known in the West in the middle of the last century.

Krishna dictated the *Bhagavad-gita* to Arjuna. It is as important for Hindus as the Gospel is for Christians.

The *Vedas*

The Hindu religion is centred around a series of hymns known as the *Vedas*, meaning knowledge. They praise the gods and are believed to have been taught to sages long ago by the gods themselves. The hymns date from 1,500 BC and are the most ancient texts in the world. They were passed down by story-tellers who knew them by heart, and were finally written down, in Sanskrit, around the 8th century BC. Centuries later a number of further writings, explaining and clarifying the *Vedas* were produced. The best-known among these are the *Upanishads* and the *Brahmana*.

The *Mahabharata*

This is the longest known epic poem, with 90,000 couplets (two-line verses). Created by various authors between the 4th century BC and the 4th century AD, it is an encyclopedia of Indian civilisation and a guide to wisdom. Hindus call it the *Fifth Veda*. The *Bhagavad-gita*, another important Hindu text, is part of it.

The *Ramayana*

This is probably the most popular of all the Hindu texts and has been passed on by word of mouth for centuries. There are versions in the language of every region. The oldest, a long epic poem of 24,000 couplets written in Sanskrit (the language of classical India in which all the sacred texts are written), is that composed by Valmiki.

The most well-known version of the *Ramayana* was written in Hindi at the end of the 16th century by the poet Tulsi-das.

Rama and Hanuman (temple of Kanchipuram).

The time of the *Vedas*

From around 2,500 BC, a great civilisation grew up in the valley of the river Indus (which gave India its name). Its cities, like Mohenjo-daro, were large and wealthy. Written tablets have been found from that time, but until recently no-one was able to read them. This society was no longer very powerful by 1,750 BC.

Around the same time, tribes from the Iranian highlands and the steppes of central Asia settled on the banks of the river Indus. These people, known as Aryans, lived very much in contact with the natural world. They believed the elements were gods and sang hymns in their praise. These holy songs developed over time into the *Vedas*, and this civilisation became known as the Vedic era.

Above: the Great Goddess Adya Kali was venerated from prehistoric times (18th-century painting).

The caste system gained importance around the 5th century BC. The first caste is that of Brahmins, who study sacred texts and practice religious rituals. The second is that of Kshatriya, kings and warriors. Third are the Vaishya, traders and farmers. Fourth are Shudra, or servants, and last – outside the castes – are untouchables.

Vedic gods

All natural things were worshipped: the earth, water, plants, trees... Indra was the thunder god; Varuna was master of the elements; Vayu was god of the wind (and Hanuman's father); Surya was the sun god. Agni, the god of fire, was venerated as the oldest of all, for he represented the sacrificial fire; Yama was god of death and of dharma. At first all the gods were equal, but soon the idea developed that everything in the world was part of one thing. As one *Veda* puts it: "He is one, but the sages give him many names."

The time of the *Ramayana*

By the 6th century BC three central gods were worshipped: Brahma who is the creator of the Universe, Vishnu the protector and Shiva the destroyer. The *Ramayana* is written in praise of Vishnu.

Centre: the god Ganesha. In his hand he holds the tusk he broke off in order to write the *Mahabharata* as the sage Vyasa dictated it to him.

Orange: Indus civilisation
Pink and green: Vedic civilisation

Indian warrior, 2nd century BC.

Sarasvati, goddess of knowledge, of words and of music, with the wild goose she rides. She holds a vina and the sacred texts (from a 19th-century painting).

Indian and South-East Asian theatre, as well as the shadow plays and puppet shows of Java, Bali, Cambodia and Thailand, have always borrowed from the *Ramayana*.

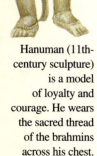

Hanuman (11th-century sculpture) is a model of loyalty and courage. He wears the sacred thread of the brahmins across his chest.

The *Ramayana* and the arts

The *Ramayana* has inspired poets and artists throughout India and South-East Asia. The many plays and festivals still performed and held today in honour of Rama testify to the power of this story.

The kathakali

From words meaning katha, story, and kali, dancing game, it is a form of theatre combining song, dance, pantomime and music. It began in Kerala, in South-West India: the Zamorin of Calicut created a new dance in honour of Krishna, but refused to let the Rajah of a neighbouring state see it. The latter replied to this insult by creating his own dance in honour of Rama. This was the Ramanattam or Deeds of Rama, told in Malayalam (the language of Kerala) so that everyone in the land could follow it.

The actors wear richly embroidered costumes and elaborate make-up to make them look like gods. The play unfolds through the night, by the light of an oil lamp before an awestruck audience, and may not finish much before dawn.

Festivals in honour of Rama

Each year, in the North of India, the festival of Ram-Lila takes place.

During September, from one full moon to the next, thousands of people gather to watch scenes from the Hindi text of the *Ramayana*, by Tulsi-das. Celebrations begin the day before the full moon, so that they are well underway by the birthday of the god-hero which is on the full moon itself.

Centre: characters from a Javanese shadow play. The figure on the left is the giant Kumbhakarna, brother of Ravana.

Above: Rama fighting on Hanuman's shoulders. (Detail from the walls of the temple at Angkor-Vat, Cambodia, early 12th century.)

Left: Rama, Sita and Lakshmana during their exile in the forest (18th-century miniature).

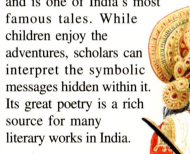

In the temples, along the Ganges and in private houses the story is told. It is even broadcast through the streets by loud-speakers. The audience plays an active part in the enactment of this drama. All together they follow Rama's chariot as he goes into exile; they are guests at his wedding and cheer his return.

In Mysore, the feast of Dusserah celebrates the victory of the gods over the forces of evil. Splendid processions and plays tell of Rama's fight against Ravana.

In the temples

Although there are countless statues of Rama and other characters from the story, few temples are dedicated to him. The most important are in Ramachandra (built around the beginning of the 16th century) and Vijayanagar (Karnataka), which is thought to be Kishkindha, the ancient city of the monkeys. One hundred and eight sculptures illustrating the story decorate the temple.

On the Indonesian island of Java, the temple of Prambanam (late 9th century) is decorated with scenes from the *Ramayana*. Between May and October, around the full moon, a ballet of the story is performed, lasting four nights.

Rameshvaram, known as the city of lord Rama, attracts most pilgrims. It was on this small island, between India and Sri Lanka, that Rama is thought to have purified himself after killing Ravana. Here he placed a lingam, a tall stone representing the creative power of the creator, in honour of Shiva.

On the screen

In 1987 Ramanand Sagar made a television serial based on Tulsi-das' *Ramayana*. Shown on Sunday mornings over a year, it proved a great success throughout India.

For young and old

The *Ramayana* has been loved by children and adults alike for centuries and is one of India's most famous tales. While children enjoy the adventures, scholars can interpret the symbolic messages hidden within it. Its great poetry is a rich source for many literary works in India.

Look out for other titles in this series:

SARAH, WHO LOVED LAUGHING
A TALE FROM THE BIBLE

THE SECRETS OF KAIDARA
AN ANIMIST TALE FROM AFRICA

I WANT TO TALK TO GOD
A TALE FROM ISLAM

THE RIVER GODDESS
A TALE FROM HINDUISM

CHILDREN OF THE MOON
YANOMAMI LEGENDS

I'LL TELL YOU A STORY
TALES FROM JUDAISM

THE PRINCE WHO BECAME A BEGGAR
A BUDDHIST TALE

JESUS SAT DOWN AND SAID...
THE PARABLES OF JESUS

SAINT FRANCIS, THE MAN WHO SPOKE TO BIRDS
TALES OF ST FRANCIS OF ASSISI

THE MAGIC OF CHRISTMAS
CHRISTMAS TALES FROM EUROPE

MUHAMMAD'S NIGHT JOURNEY
A TALE FROM ISLAM

WHEN BRENDAN DISCOVERED PARADISE
A CHRISTIAN TALE FROM IRELAND